Aerola's BIG TRIP

Aerola's BIG TRIP

written by
Ramona Moscatello, Lathanise Moscatello, & Lakawthra Cox

illustrated by
Erin Cox

Library of Congress Control Number: 2020917797
          Paperback: 978-1-958169-04-9
          eBook: 978-1-958169-05-6

Printed in the United States of America

Thank God for our talents.

We dedicate this book to our family and friends.

Aerola Bombus, a bumblebee, was born in the state of Washington on the petals of a pretty rhododendron. One day when she had grown, she carried pollen from flower to flower. Flowers need bees and insects to transfer pollen from one flower to another, so that flowers will continue to grow. She was bored from carrying pollen over and over. Although the state of Washington contained beautiful hills and rivers, she wanted to fly farther and see more of the United States.

Aerola's first stop landed in Utah on a sego lily. Guess what was on that lily, a new red hat! Aerola was so surprised that her eyes turned green!

In Missouri, she traded her red hat for a queen's crown. She won it by pollinating the most hawthorns in one day. They declared Aerola, "Queen Bee for the Day!"

While visiting Indiana, Aerola pollinated a pink peony. She loved it so much that she traded the crown for a pink wig and her new friends called her *Peony.*

The blustery winds of North Dakota blew her pretty wig into South Dakota and chapped her lips. Aerola obtained lip-gloss from a wild prairie rose in North Dakota before fluttering to Ohio.

Aerola bought a yellow shirt in Ohio so that she could look like the sun. She thought it would help the scarlet carnations bloom brighter. She stayed an extra day to visit a large white trillium. While there, she bought a new shirt and a magician's hat.

Aerola used her magician's hat to *poof* her to New York. She also wished for a pretty pink bow, which was so pretty that she gave away her magician's hat. The bow reminded her of the beautiful New York rose.

Next, Aerola traveled to Tennessee to visit her grandparents. She picked an iris as a present for her grandmother. She gave her grandfather a purple passion flower for his birthday. He hadn't been feeling well, and the flower pepped him up. Her grandmother and grandfather gave her a hug and a kiss.

With good feelings from their kisses and hugs, Aerola zipped over to Oklahoma. Oklahoma's state insect, the honeybee, was abundant. While relaxing on an Oklahoma rose, Aerola made many friends and ate lots of honey. She saved a jug of honey for her next trip.

A cold gust of wind reminded her that she would soon have to hibernate. Before leaving Oklahoma, she pollinated an Indian blanket flower. She grabbed two of its petals to keep her warm for when she hibernates.

Before winter Aerola made one more stop. She visited her cousin, Apian, in Texas. Apian taught her to dance the Texas Two-Step. The bees danced two steps to the left, two steps to the right, and then hopped from one buffalo clover to the next.

Aerola and Apian took a break and ate honey from Aerola's jug. Then the bees covered themselves using Indian blanket petals. Aerola rested before flying back to the state of Washington. She packed three buffalo clover petals to use as pillows for when she hibernates in Washington.

In preparation for cold weather, Aerola headed to Washington with her honey, Indian blanket petals, and three buffalo clover petals to hibernate.

Upon reaching Washington, Aerola Bombus headed to Yakima Park to find well-drained soil. There she found a fallen log and burrowed in the ground underneath the log to sleep. While sleeping in her burrow, she dreamed about where she would visit in the spring.

ACTIVITY

While you are outside, look for various flowers or vegetation. Write your observation in a notebook, and with the help of an adult look, online, for each flower by its characteristics. Make your own glossary of flowers from your area and state by listing the name of each flower followed by its characteristics.

Note to educators and parents: How to use this book to introduce botany, geography, and history follows.

BOTANY:

Before or after reading Aerola's adventure, take a diagram of a flower and teach children the parts of a flower. While teaching the parts of a flower, explain how pollination works. Ask the children questions, such as, "Why is pollination important?" Lastly, discuss what flowers need to grow and explain photosynthesis. As Aerola encounters each flower, discuss the characteristics of each flower.

GEOGRAPHY:

When Aerola encounters a state, use her encounters to discuss the latitudinal and longitudinal lines of each state. Use a globe to locate each state, while explaining the definition of latitudinal and longitudinal lines. Introduce the general directions of north, south, east, and west. As Aerola enters a new state, ask the children the general direction of that state in relation to the entire United States. Also discuss geographical features of the states, such as, "Oklahoma has rolling plains."

HISTORY:

Aerola's adventures can introduce the history of each state. As Aerola enters a state, discuss when that state became part of the U.S. Use the glossary to discuss when the state flower became official.

GLOSSARY

The scientific or proper names are in parentheses.

Aero: air or atmosphere.

Apian: relating to bees or having characteristic of bees.

Blue Bonnet: (*Lupinus subcarnous*) Also known as the Buffalo Clover; Texas state flower.

Buffalo Clover: (*Lupinus subcarnous*) Also known as the Blue Bonnet; Texas state flower.

Bombus: (*Bombus pennsylvanicus*) Scientific name for bumblebee.

Hawthorns: (*Crataegus spp.*) Floral emblem for Missouri.

Indiana: Located in the eastern part of north central region of the United States and the 19th state of the United States.

Indian Blanket: (*Gaillardia pulchella*) Oklahoma state wildflower.

Iris: (*Family Iridaceae*) State flower of Tennessee.

Missouri: Located in the Midwest region of the United States and the 24th state of the United States.

New York: Located in the northeast region of the United States and the 11th state of the United States.

New York Rose: (*Rosa*) The rose is the New York State Flower. Any combination or colors of or common rose satisfy as the New York state flower.

North Dakota: Located in the western north-central United States and became the 39th state of the United States.

Ohio: Located in the eastern part of the north-central United States and became the 17th state of the United States.

Oklahoma: Located in the south central region of the United States and became the 46th state of the United States.

Oklahoma Rose: (*Rosa ordoata- Andr. Sweet*) Oklahoma state flower since 2004.

Pink Peony: (*Paeonia*) Indiana state flower, although not native to the state.

Pollen: Fine powder produced by certain plants when they reproduce.

Pollination: The transfer of pollen from an anther to the stigma in angiosperms or from the microsporangium to the micropyle in gymnosperms.

Pretty Rhonodendron: (*Rhodendron macrophyllum*) Washington Flower.

Purple Passion: (*Passiflora incarnate*) Tennessee state wildflower

Scarlet Carnation: (*Genus Dianthus caryophyllus*) Ohio state flower.

Sego Lily: (*Calochortus nuttallii Torr. & Gray*) Utah state flower.

South Dakota: Located in the western front of the north central region of the United States and the 40th state of the United States.

Tennessee: Located in the east south central region of the United States and the 16th state that of the United States.

Texas: Located in the south central region of the United States and the 28th state of the United States.

Utah: Located in the west central region of the United States and the 45th state of the United States.

Washington: Located in the pacific northwest region of the United States and the 42nd state of the United States.

White Trillium (Large): (*Trillium grandiflorum*) Also known as the great white trillium, wake-robin, and snow trillium. Ohio State Wild Flower.

Wild Prairie Rose: (*Rosa blanda*) North Dakota State Flower.